Meet My Mom

Learning the M Sound

Sharon Moore

Phonics for the REAL World™

Rosen Classroom Books and Materials™
New York

Meet my mom.

My mom takes me to school.

My mom goes to work.

My mom meets me after school.

SENECA CENTRAL

My mom and I make dinner.

My mom helps me mop the mess.

My mom and I make a map.

MAP
Our House

My mom and I play.

My mom reads to me.

My mom gives me a hug.

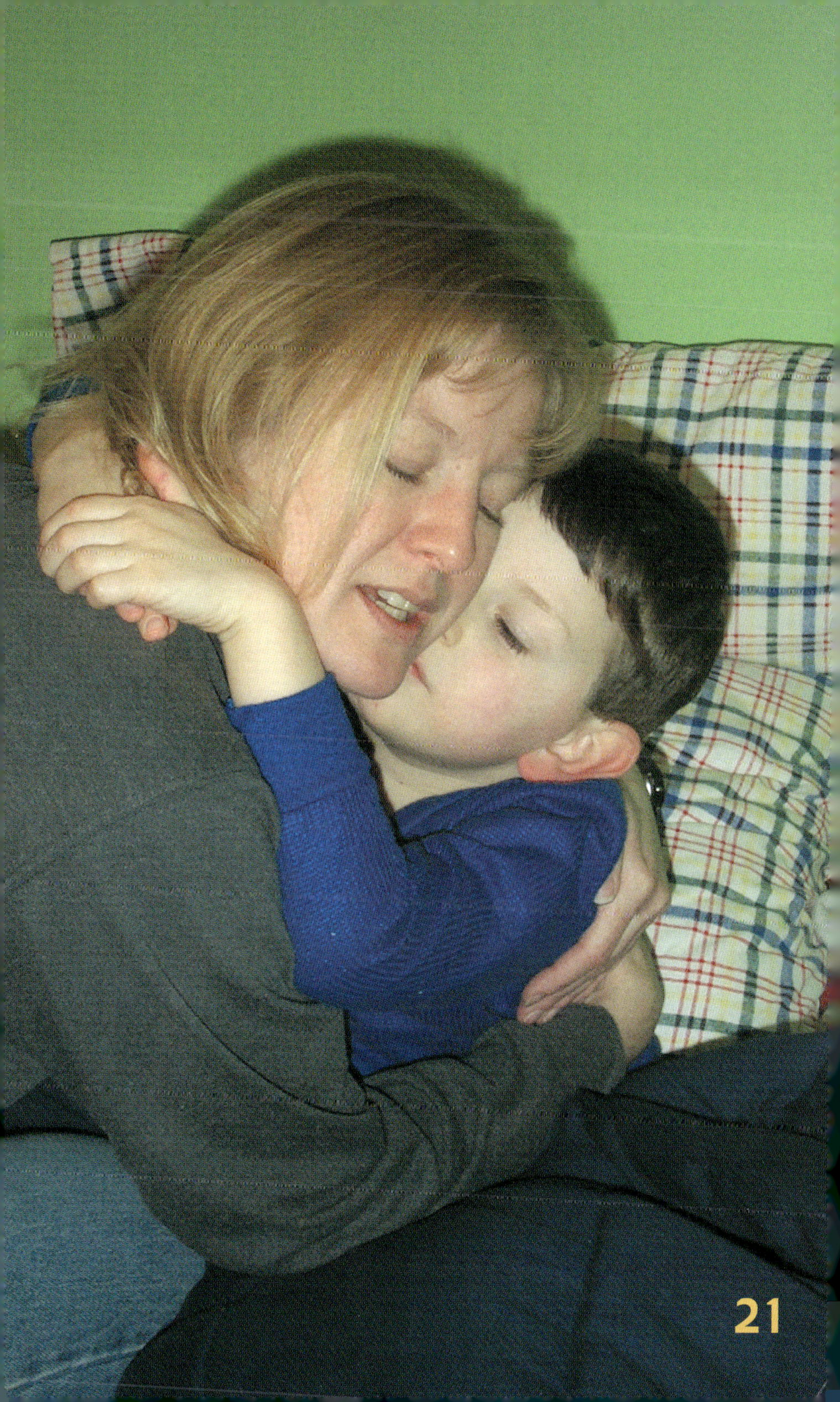

Word List

make

map

me

meet

mess

mom

mop

my

Instructional Guide

Note to Instructors:
One of the essential skills that enable a young child to read is the ability to associate letter-sound symbols and blend these sounds to form words. Phonics instruction can teach children a system that will help them decode unfamiliar words and, in turn, enhance their word-recognition skills. We offer a phonics-based series of books that are easy to read and understand. Each book pairs words and pictures that reinforce specific phonetic sounds in a logical sequence. Topics are based on curriculum goals appropriate for early readers in the areas of science, social studies, and health.

Letter/Sound: m – Display four drawings or magazine pictures, three of objects beginning with **m**, one with a different sound. Ask the child to name the pictures and select the three that begin with consonant sound **m**. Write each word and ask the child to underline the initial **m**. Continue with other sets of pictures.

Phonics Activities: Place several of the picture cards used to introduce the beginning **m** sound on a mat. After discussing the pictures, cover the display with a cloth. Ask the child to recall as many of them as they can. Encourage them to use complete sentences. *(On the mat, I saw a monkey, a muffin, and a mitten.)* Write the names of the items and ask the child to underline the initial **m** in each word. Ask the child to close their eyes while you remove an item from the collection on the mat. Have the child state which item is missing, using a complete sentence. *(The mug is missing from the mat.)* (Suggestions for **m** words: *mop, mail, meat, mask, milk, men, monkey, moon.*)

- Ask the child to solve rhyme riddles about the items on the mat. (Example: *It begins with* ***m*** *and rhymes with silk. What is it?*) After the child responds, write the riddle answer and point out the initial **m**. Follow up by having the child create their own riddles.

Additional Resources:

- Arno, Iris H. *I Love You, Mom*. Mahwah, NJ: Troll Communications L.L.C., 1998.
- Black, Sonia W. *Hanging Out with Mom*. New York: Scholastic, Inc., 1997.
- Kaplan, John. *Mom & Me*. New York: Scholastic, Inc., 1997.
- Schaefer, Lola M. *Mothers*. Mankato, MN: Capstone Press, Inc., 1999.

Published in 2002 by The Rosen Publishing Group, Inc.
29 East 21st Street, New York, NY 10010

Book Design: Haley Wilson

Photo Credits: All pictures by Karey Schuckers-Churley

Library of Congress Cataloging-in-Publication Data

Moore, Sharon.
Meet my mom : learning the M sound / Sharon Moore.—1st ed.
p. cm. — (Power phonics/phonics for the real world)
ISBN 0-8239-5913-9 (lib. bdg.)
ISBN 0-8239-8258-0 (pbk.)
6-pack ISBN 0-8239-9226-8
1. Mother and child—Juvenile literature. 2. Mothers—Juvenile literature. [1. Mother and child. 2. Mothers.] I. Title. II. Series.

HQ755.85 .M65 2002
306.874'3—dc21

00-013160

Manufactured in the United States of America